COSMOPOLITAN

COMPLETE SATISFACTION

OVER 300 EARTH-SHATTERING SEX TIPS

THIS IS A CARLTON BOOK
Text, design and illustrations copyright © 2005
Carlton Books Limited
This edition published by Carlton Books Limited 2005
20 Mortimer Street, London W1T 3JW

Material for this book has previously appeared under the Cosmopolitan
titles *Sexercise: Over 100 Truly Explosive Tips* (Carlton, 2002), *Over
100 Truly Astonishing Sex Tips* (Carlton, 2000) and *Over 100 Triple X
Sex Tricks* (Carlton, 2005).

ISBN 1 84442 452 9

Printed and bound in Singapore

Executive Editor: Lisa Dyer
Senior Art Editor: Zoë Dissell
Designers: Michelle Pickering, DW Design and Nicole Le Grange
Illustrator: Nicola Slater
Production: Caroline Alberti

COSMOPOLITAN

COMPLETE SATISFACTION

OVER 300 EARTH-SHATTERING SEX TIPS

SUSSMAN

CARLTON BOOKS

CONTENTS

SEXERCISE:
TRULY EXPLOSIVE TIPS

WEEK ONE: RECIPES FOR LUST

Your brain may be your most important sexual organ, but there's no getting around the fact that lovemaking gets better when the rest of your body is in shape. Studies on the relationship between sensational sex and health keep coming up with the same finding: just like keeping your car in tip-top condition, the key to a really good sex life (i.e., one that includes not just regular but teeth-rattling orgasms) is proper maintenance.

This isn't about transforming yourself into the female Schwarzenegger; it's about discovering and toning little-known muscles and hormones that contribute to more intense, enjoyable, even transcendent lovemaking for both of you.

The best news is, all it takes to improve your sex life forever is five short weeks. Think you have what it takes to enter the winner's circle? Then look no further for a get-fit plan that will keep you coming – and coming back for more.

Let the games begin!

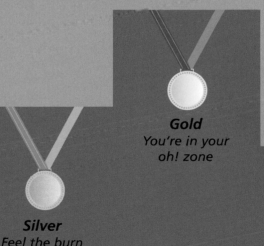

Gold
You're in your
oh! zone

Silver
Feel the burn

Bronze
Heavy breathing

HORMONE HEAVEN

Getting a grip on your menstrual cycle will help you get the most out of it as a love machine.

Rejoice when your period comes – and not just because it means you're not pregnant. Science has found that those monthly changes in your levels of oestrogen and its sister hormones are what affect the intensity of your orgasms and give you a strong, flexible vagina, and regular production of cervical and vaginal lubricants.

Another happy by-product of following your hormonal peaks is that **oestrogen** and **progesterone** are defenders against STDs within your reproductive tract (although no one's suggesting this means you should skimp on the protection).

Come autumn, **be ready for a quickie**. Hormone levels often peak in October, before they drop again at the first cold spell.

Mark these key days on your calendar:

The average length of a cycle is 28 days. Start counting from the first day of your period.

- It's day 10 and you feel marvellous, darling. Your oestrogen levels are at their pre-ovulatory peak and you are in the mood for love.

- Know where your man is on day 14. It's ovulation time which means testosterone (always present in your blood at a low level) spikes just as oestrogen crests, making you feel sexually aggressive. Your libido's raging and you're at your most man-magnetic. By the way, your body's also primed to get pregnant right now, so don't forget contraception!

- Day 18 and you're in seductive mode – rising levels of oxytocin, the touch hormone, trigger a lust to touch and be touched. Now! Bonus: this hormone also sets off the uterine contractions that go with orgasm.

- Make love on the 28th day of your cycle. Your brain misreads uterine puffiness as a sign of sexual arousal and actually craves orgasmic release. Wowza, wowza!

THE PHWOARGASM DIET

This no-deprivation diet will raise your ahhh-q.

5

Honey pollen stimulates reproductive systems. **Swallow the pollen** in tablet form or stir granules straight into food (use those listed in tips 6–9 for a double love whammy).

6

Phosphorus has direct impact on sexual desire. Try food enriched with the miracle mineral (almonds, scallops, cheddar cheese, wheat bran, brewer's yeast and sunflower seeds) for glow-in-the-dark pleasure.

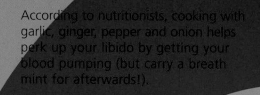

According to nutritionists, cooking with garlic, ginger, pepper and onion helps perk up your libido by getting your blood pumping (but carry a breath mint for afterwards!).

Vegetarians might just be on to something. Researchers at the US Department of Agriculture have found that the mineral **boron** is vital for hormone production and sexual function. Boron can be found in dark green leafy vegetables, fruits (not citrus), nuts and legumes.

Take your vitamins. You need 45-plus nutrients daily to maintain good health (translation: regular orgasms). Even minor deficiencies can weaken the libido. Here's what you need to stockpile for better bliss. Bon O's.

- Vitamin B (bread, yogurt): converts sugar and starches into energy, which translates into more stamina in bed.

- Vitamin E (spinach, oatmeal, asparagus, eggs, nuts, brown rice, fruit): also known as the sex vitamin, this is the one to pop to perk up passion.

- Zinc (fish, oysters, liver, mushroom, grains, fresh fruit): increases testosterone levels in men and women. University of Rochester researchers found that men with zinc-deficient diets are at high risk of low libido and sex problems like infertility and prostrate problems (his pleasure-zone gland).

- Vitamin D and calcium (milk, cheese): keep bones strong to do tricky positions without embarrassing fractures.

Go for a java jolt: a University of Michigan study found that compared to those who did not drink coffee, regular black oil drinkers were considerably more sexually active. Warning: caffeine can also deliver a performance-boosting jolt to sperm cells, increasing both their velocity (speed) and motility (liveliness).

11

Go ahead and eat that Cadbury's. Chocolate contains not only caffeine (see tip 10) but also phenylethylamine (PEA), dubbed the 'molecule of love' by sexual medicine specialist Theresa Crenshaw, MD, author of *The Alchemy of Love and Lust*. A natural form of the stimulant amphetamine, a dose of PEA can increase lust levels to red-hot (the artificial sweetener aspartame also contains PEA so for those watching their weight, a Diet Coke will have the same effect).

LOVE SABOTEURS

Not in the mood? Before blaming your partner, check out your medicine cabinet, diet, birth control and lifestyle.

12

Problem: Fatigue.

Solution: Use your bed … to sleep in, that is. Lots of sex feels great but research shows that you need a minimum of 6–8 hours sleep a night to feel energized for all that sex.

Problem: Smoking.

Solution: Kick ash. It seems that quitting the butt habit can make a bigger difference in your life than exercising. A study at the University of California at San Diego found that tobacco reduces testosterone levels and constricts blood flow, which has a less than smoking effect on your orgasms.

Problem: Contraception.

Solution: Take your pill. A study at McGill University, Montreal, found that Pill users report more frequent and more satisfactory sex than non-users. Possible reasons: lighter menstrual periods, reduced PMS, mental security against pregnancy and the spontaneity of this contraceptive method allows them to relax and enjoy the moment more. (Note: the Pill isn't for everyone – see tip 15 – and should be used WITH a condom if you aren't sure about your partner's bill of health.)

Problem: The Pill. It contains progesterone, a hormone that diminishes lubrication, sex drive and delays climax. You may still want sex and even enjoy it but the ultimate orgasmic blast-off can become a huge, labour-intensive effort. Hormonal implants can have the same effect.

Solution: Switch to triphasic pills which have different levels of progesterone and, a San Francisco State University study found, may actually even increase desire.

Problem: Your medicine prescription. Research by the Sex/Drug Interaction Foundation in California estimates that up to 20 per cent of all sex problems are caused by drug side effects or interactions. Certain asthma, blood-pressure, diabetes and migraine medications, synthetic androgens (used to treat endometriosis), heartburn soothers, antibiotics and beta blockers (used to treat cardiovascular disease) will all short-circuit desire and orgasm.

Solution: Talk to your doctor about gentler alternative treatments.

Problem: Over-the-counter sex stoppers. Antihistamines, decongestants and sleep aids are muscles relaxants – and you need muscle tension to reach orgasm. In addition, they can dry out the body's mucous membranes, making intercourse uncomfortable.

Solution: Read the label before you buy. If it says, 'May cause drowsiness', it can also impair sexual desire or performance.

Problem: Depression. Selective serotonin re-uptake inhibitors (SSRIs) – like Prozac, Zoloft and Paxil – have been found to have a downing effect on your sexuality, causing lowered libido, lack of arousal, delay in orgasm or reduction in orgasmic intensity.

Solution: A lower dose might reduce sexual side effects while preserving antidepressant effects. Or try a drug holiday (check with your doctor first). A study by MacLean Hospital in Massachusetts found that more than half of those taking antidepressants reported better sexual functioning and more desire when they had drug-free weekends (Thursday noon to Sunday noon). Also see tip 121.

19

Problem: Booze. Ironically, we drink to lower inhibition. But alcohol also lowers sex drive. A general rule of thumb is that the amount of alcohol it takes to affect your driving (for an average-size woman, one to two drinks an hour) will also affect your libido.

Solution: Get your high naturally (see tip 121).

Problem: Your diet. Big pre-thang meals can affect you in much the same way as alcohol. It makes you feel fat, sleepy, and you sweat what you eat. Lovely!

Solution: Lighten up on the heavy meals, especially those containing fatty oils and butter. See tips 5–9 for dishes that'll keep you purring with pleasure.

X20

Problem: His knickers. Besides studies showing that tight briefs might affect his sperm count, lower back moves while wearing tight gym shorts can result in a painful swelling known as stretcher's scrotum.

Solution: Make sure he hangs loose at all times.

Problem: He's a cyclist. Too much wheeling can result in Alcock Syndrome (numb willy from too much bicycle riding).

Solution: Help him get his exercise in other ways (like lying down).

GET NATURAL

Additive free doses of desire.*

Gingko biloba
WHAT IT DOES: Several studies have found that
it improves blood flow throughout the body by
relaxing arteries, aiding potency in men and
orgasmic release in women.
DOSE: Start at 80 mg per day.

Ginseng
WHAT IT DOES: This herb contains ginsenosides,
compounds that researchers think can improve
sexual function by encouraging the body to make
more testosterone.
DOSE: 2 g per day. Be sure to check the label for
the designation Panax, which means that the herb
is of American or Oriental origin (the most reliable).
It's also important to buy a standardized formula
containing 15 per cent ginsenosides; that means
the manufacturers have tested the product to
ensure that there are sufficient quantities of the
active ingredient.

*Warning: You may have to take these herbs for several weeks
before you see any results. Let your doctor know what you're
taking to avoid interactions with other medications and never
take any herbs if you are pregnant.

Avena sativa

WHAT IT DOES: This green oat straw has been a staple of sex formulas because it may help alleviate sexual problems (especially low libido) by raising testosterone levels. In one study, 20 men who took the extract reported a 54 per cent increase in frequency of sexual activity.

DOSE: 300 mg per day

St John's wort

WHAT IT DOES: A natural antidepressant, it is also thought to be a natural libido lifter. Warning: It's been found to decrease the effectiveness of the Pill.

DOSE: 900 mg per day of a 0.3 per cent standardized extract.

Damiana

WHAT IT DOES: This herb has a long-standing reputation as a sexual stimulant. It contains volatile oils that stimulate nerve endings and increase circulation to the genitals.

DOSE: Steep two teaspoons of fried damiana leaves in one cup of water and drink three times a day.

2

WEEK TWO: THE LOVE WORKOUT

Ever tried a new position, only to find that while the mind is willing, the thighs are screaming, 'How long do you expect me to keep this up?' Unlike most full-contact sports, you can't call time-out during lovemaking. Which is why trimming the flab, toning muscles and building stamina are vital to getting good sex (good hygiene and ace blow job skills don't hurt either). An orgasm is essentially a series of contractions of the uterine, vaginal, rectal and pubococcygeus (PC) muscles. Ergo, the stronger your muscles, the stronger the contractions, the more pleasure you'll feel and the more control you'll have over your own – and your lover's – bliss.

All it takes is 20 minutes of exercise a week to develop killer love muscles. Keep it moderate (around 145 heartbeats per minute) or you'll be too whacked to get whacked. Expect results within weeks.

One word of caution all you A-type personalities: take it easy. In the sex/exercise connection, more isn't better (good news). Too much muscle soreness and fatigue can easily put a damper on romance while over-rigorous training can cause hormonal imbalances in your libido. Three times a week is more than enough to feel results.

JUST DO IT

It's official: A hard body leads to better whoa!

It starts with the heart. In a study of nearly 3,000 men and women by the University of California at San Diego, it was found that as fitness levels improve, so does cardiovascular endurance. This means a greater volume of blood can be pumped throughout the body – genitals included. And blood circulation is key for a man's erection and a woman's arousal system (it increases lubrication and clitoral swelling). Kinda makes you want to check out those step classes after all, huh?

28

29

Don't be afraid to break a sweat – perspiration is actually an aphrodisiac packed with come-hither-and-ravage-me pheromones (up the stakes by chucking away your deodorant). In Shakespeare's time, a woman hoping to attract a man tucked a peeled apple in her armpit and then offered this 'love apple' to the object of her lust.

Another reason to skip your **post-workout shower** and steam up in bed instead: exercise also stimulates the endocrine glands, making testosterone levels in both men and women rise sharply. Translation: you want it and you want it now.

Additional bonus: if you're healthy and in good shape, you may climax more easily. Sex therapist Dr Linda De Villers studied more than 8,000 women and found regular exercisers had more intense and fulfilling orgasms – perhaps because people who workout take pride in their bodies and have higher self-esteem. (It's harder to have an orgasm if you're obsessing over the size of your bum.)

If the above still hasn't made you jump on a treadmill, consider this: pumping it up also gets you in shape for your own tour de sex. Regular aerobic activity – such as cycling, swimming, jogging or stepping on a Stairmaster – improves cardiovascular endurance, which translates to **more staying power in the bedroom**.

And don't forget the **curative powers** of exercise. For years, women who had problems with sex drive, arousal or orgasm were told to relax and take a bubble bath. But research from the University of Texas at Austin suggests the opposite is true: women should do something arousing to get stimulated – like working out. Get revved. Time to renew that gym membership?

4

Stay motivated with this news: A study at the University of Texas in Austin found that **working out makes you horny**. When you exercise, heart rate and blood pressure are elevated and the blood vessels in the genitals become primed for action. Result: post-workout sex is bound to be explosive (see tips 30–33 for more erotic incentive).

Finally, exercise keeps nerves in tip-top shape, sharpening the ability to feel and **focus on all bodily sensations** (and tune out that annoying 'Did I pay the electricity bill?' voice). Continue toning exercises during your lovemaking for the ultimate sensual experience!

35

Don't leave him on the couch: after nine months of working out for one hour three times a week, your man is likely to have a shorter post-ejaculation recovery period. Hello, orgasmic hat tricks!

Don't leave him on the couch 2: The American Council on Exercise reports that burning at least 200 calories a day exercising (the equivalent of walking two miles briskly) can keep his willy perky and interested, preventing or even reversing premature ejaculation, low libido and penile droop.

SWEAT IT OUT

Key cardio moves for getting hot and bothered.

Alternate your aerobic days with a weight-training regimen that covers the full body – arms, legs, abdomen, chest and back (see tips 48–51, 55, 56 and 83 for ideas). Use either free weights or a weight machine system like Nautilus. The goal is to **increase strength and tone muscles**, so work with a weight that's about half of what you're capable of lifting. Do three sets of 12 repetitions for each muscle group.

Start pounding the pavement. In one poll, 66 per cent of the men and women runners interviewed claimed that regular jogging made them better lovers.

Or **put a spin** on your workouts. In another poll, two-thirds of bicycling enthusiasts said cycling made them better lovers.

Lap it up for long-lasting juiciness. A Harvard University study of middle-aged swimmers concluded that men and women over 40 who got wet regularly were as sexually active as people in their late twenties and early thirties. And they enjoyed it more.

42

For explosive results, go from almost no exercise to three one-hour workouts a week. One study found that this technique results in a 30 per cent increase in how often you play the field, a 20 per cent increase in tonsil hockey and a decrease in being benched because of non-working parts.

Insider tip: you don't have to schedule a gym trip every time you want to have sex. The kind of breathlessness necessary for a **precoital charge** can also be had from a rowdy, bawdy pillow fight with your lover. Tickling, wrestling and fighting can all also set off sparks.

43

PELVIS POWER

Forget upper arms as taut as cables and a bum so firm you can flip a coin off of it – the stronger your and his pelvic muscles are, the tighter you'll both be able to contract during sex and squeeze out every last drop of pleasure (see tips 77–81 for more on how to apply penile pressure).

Libido lifter: Lie flat with your arms at your sides, knees bent and feet flat on the floor. Raise your hips as high as you can and hold for a count of three, then lower them until your body nearly touches the floor. Do triple sets of ten three times a week for pumping endurance that a WWF wrestler would envy.

The thrust: A variation of tip 44. Lie down as before, then raise your hips so your bum is the only part of your body off the floor. Slowly rock or tilt your pelvis up while exhaling and down while inhaling. Repeat slowly and smoothly 20 times.

The tilt: Open the muscles of the pelvic floor by getting down on all fours with your hands directly beneath your shoulders and your knees under your hips. On a long, slow inhalation, lower your belly and lift your pelvis, then look towards the ceiling. On the exhalation, arch your back upwards, drop your head and tuck your tailbone forward. Slowly and smoothly alternate between these poses for about 30 seconds, focusing on the movement in your pelvis.

Rock-and-roll: Stand and swivel your hips, doing a rolling motion as if you're doing a bad Elvis imitation. Move only your hips, not your shoulders or upper body. Do this for one or two minutes at various speeds once or twice a day.

LIFT IT

Before you do the limbo of love, beef up with these never-gruelling-always-gratifying strength-training moves that target your erotic core. (Don't worry – they take longer to read than to actually do.)

Shoulders: To keep you in shape for staying on top (which is, incidentally, the best position to stimulate the G-spot and other sensitive areas in the vagina, such as its end).

WORK IT: Sit up. Hold your arms above your head and cross your wrists. Inhale, straightening your arms. Extend them back behind your head as far as possible, keeping your wrists crossed (your elbows should be behind your ears). Hold for ten seconds, then relax. Repeat three times.

MIX IT IN: See tips 83, 84 and 91.

Upper arms: Strengthening the triceps will help you hold yourself up longer when you're on top (see tip 48 for why you want to be on top).

WORK IT: Sit on a chair with its back against a wall, holding the front of the seat with the heels of your hands. Slide off the chair and freeze, with your knees bent, elbows facing the wall and arms supporting your body. Lower your body, bending your elbows to a 90° angle, then push up. Do 3 sets of 15.

MIX IT IN: See tips 83, 89 and 92.

Abdominals: These are your orgasmic power centre. They help maintain your position, push your inner clitoris into the path of his penis, keep the lower back strong (important for those sexy thrusts) and hold your belly in (important when it comes to luring a partner to willingly do the aforementioned thrusting motions with you).

WORK IT: Sit up straight. Pull your belly button in for one second, imagining it's touching the back of your spine. Release. Repeat 99 times, counting aloud (so you don't hold your breath). Aim for five sets of 100 a day.

MIX IT IN: Squeeze your abs during sex – you'll beef up your orgasms to twice their usual size (see tips 85 and 88 for more fabdominal ideas).

Derrière: Strengthening these muscles helps build pressure in your pelvic region – which will feel incredible when released.

WORK IT: Flex and release your bum rhythmically for about 20 seconds every day.

MIX IT IN: Clenching your buns together every couple of seconds during sex will push you both over the Big O brink (see tip 95 for more yum-bum moves).

52

Back: Sex feels better than busting concrete, but your back muscles don't know the difference. Sex-related backaches are especially common when nearing climax, the point of maximum muscle tension.

WORK IT: Lie on your back and slowly bring your knees to your chest. Grab your knees and hold them against your chest for a few breaths, relaxing throughout the movement.

MIX IT IN: Elevate your legs by lying flat on the floor and propping your feet on the backs of his thighs during sex. This will take the pressure off the sciatic nerve and relax those hot twinges of a minor backache. Tips 84 and 88 will also make you sit straight with pleasure.

Hips: Don't forget to hit below the belt. As the key pivot in the thrusting motion, your hip joints and muscles must remain flexible.

WORK IT: Push both thighs outwards and hold for thirty seconds. Relax. Repeat ten times.

MIX IT IN: Get on top – it's an instant hip easer (see tip 83 for muscle workers to stay on top).

53

54

Inner thighs:
Necessary for those tricky standing-on-one-leg-on-a-tree-limb moves.

WORK IT: Sit on a chair and squeeze your knees, pushing them together for about ten seconds. Repeat ten times, three times a day.

MIX IT IN: Do the squeeze during the missionary position – you'll create friction on the outer part of the clitoris and the inner folds of the vulva – yum!

55

Upper thighs: The quads – the muscles at the front of the thighs – are key players in any on-top position (see tip 48 for why you want to train for this position).

WORK IT: Stand 30 cm (1 ft) away from a wall, facing out. Lean back so your torso touches the wall. Slide down, bending your knees until your thighs are parallel to the floor. Hold for 30 seconds, building up to two minutes.

MIX IT IN: Check tip 96 to put these muscles in use.

56

Calves: This move stops you from overflexing your calf muscles during orgasm (and ending up with the wrong kind of spasms).

WORK IT: Lie flat on your back with one leg bent and one leg straight. Raise the straight leg as far as you can until it's pointing at the ceiling. Hold and exhale while slowly flexing your foot, pointing the toes down towards your chest. Relax, then lower the leg. Repeat three times on each leg.

MIX IT IN: Lock your legs around his hips and squeeze your calves, drawing him closer.

Brain: This is your main love muscle, so go for the golden goal and keep it strong.

WORK IT: Fantasize, dream up new scenarios and ways to touch him.

MIX IT IN: Share the above with your lover.

57

WEEK THREE: THE JOY OF FLEX

It's not enough to be strong. You also want to be limber and loose. Studies have found that muscle tightness dramatically blocks the range of motion of the legs, hips and pelvis – all key players in sexual activity. In addition, most of us clench our muscles when aroused, trying to almost push ourselves into coming.

On the flip side, stretching pumps a lot of blood into muscles and that stimulates the nerves that run through them. And when you can relax and go slack and submit to ecstasy, your orgasm will simply come to you.

These stretches and breathing exercises will help you loosen up for every tight spot you want to get in. Designed to stretch and tone AND make you both moan, these should be done two or three times weekly to stay permanently loose or within several hours of a planned rendezvous to help you soar to a more aware and prolonged state of arousal.

58 GET A BUZZ ON

Breathe your way to erotic bliss.

To make it through the long haul, long-distance runners must learn to master their breathing. And if you want to make medal-winning moves on your mattress, you should do the same. Breathe deeply through your mouth, all the way down to your diaphragm. Once you have a rhythm going, speed it up breath by breath to raise the level of sexual excitement and push you over the finishing line.

Learn the seven chakra breaths. Inhale deeply so that your lower belly expands. Exhale slowly and fully, using the abdominal muscles to expel all of the air from the lungs. With each complete breath (inhale plus exhale), focus on the base of your spine (strength), uterus (sexuality), stomach (emotions), heart (love), throat (expression), forehead (intuition), and crown (individuality). This will open up all the places where there's tension, enhancing sensitivity, allowing pleasure in, heightening sexual perceptions and increasing stamina. Make love immediately after doing this – it's more likely you'll have a whole body orgasm.

This only works when you know you're **about to get lucky**. Plug your left nostril for fifteen minutes prior to the action starting and you'll increase the air flow to the sexier side of the brain, which really gets you in the mood. Of course, that tissue dangling from your nose might kill it.

Share a Tantric kiss: Sit on his lap. Inhale while he's exhaling. As he breathes out, you'll suck his breath into your body, down to your sex organs. After one minute, kiss and share your breath. Intercourse may not even be necessary when you're so merged.

STRETCH YOURSELF SEXY

Prepare for passion with these lusty moves to improve your let-me-at-him lunges.

Imagine the **positions you want** to get in for lovemaking and do them as stretches. Hold the pose, breathing deeply and stretching just a little more with each exhale.

The psoas muscle is central for **rocking the pelvis forward** and back and side to side – moves that turn sex into an ooh-la-la experience. Strengthen yours with this yoga stretch. Stand with your knees slightly bent and inhale while gently rocking your pelvis back. Exhale as you smoothly return to your original position. Your weight should remain evenly balanced on your feet.

Shake your booty. During conventional orgasms, muscles get so charged and tense that they need release, and the experience is over. Standing and shaking out your body for 10 minutes, part by part, will let out tension and get energy flowing throughout your entire body, getting you ready for tip 95.

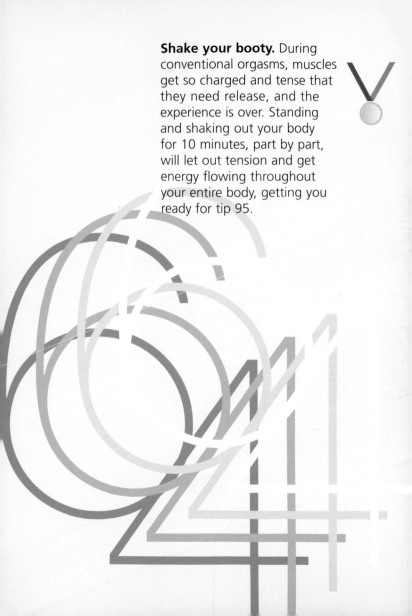

Release your inner groin muscles and shake hands with deeper, more fulfilling orgasms. Sit with your legs wide apart. Bring the soles of your feet together, resting on the outside of each foot. Draw your feet towards your pelvis and gently press their soles together to increase the stretch. Hold and breathe for one to two minutes.

Kneel with your **bottom on your feet**. Lean forward, resting your torso on the top of your thighs and stretching your arms out in front of you to loosen the muscles along your spine. Have your partner stand directly behind you and gently press your back to enhance the stretch. Switch places and repeat. This will loosen your upper, middle and lower back, making it easier to have an orgasmic triathlon (now try tips 93 and 96).

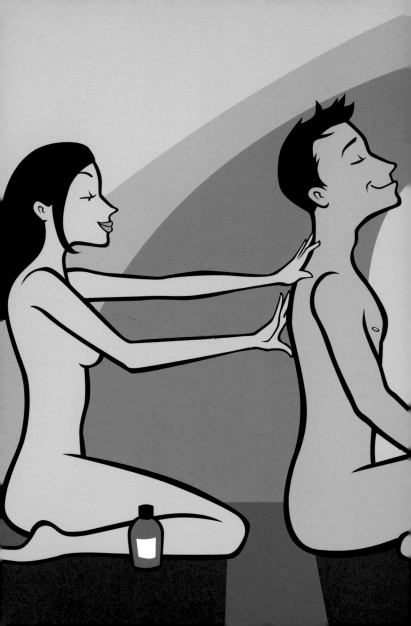

Get a quick lift when you feel drained by lowering your head, flipping your hair forward and pressing on the back of your head. This area is your energy zone and stretching it boosts circulation (the secret to all good orgasms). Extra pick-you-up-and-push-you-over-the-edge tip: spritz the area with a sharp, spicy fragrance containing musk or ylang ylang.

Knead out those knots. A sensual massage will turn up the body heat in more ways than one. Athletes get massages to increase circulation to the muscle groups. The increased blood flow warms the muscles so they'll stretch more easily and perform to their fullest capacity. To ensure personal-best sexual performance, dab a few drops of massage oil or lotion on your hands and place them, palms flat, on your partner's lower back. Run your palms in small circles up his back, along both sides of his spine, all the way up to his shoulders. Have him do the same for you. Then slip yourselves into tip 97.

GET SPIRITUAL

Shape up with this no-sweat Tantric workout. For best results, follow it step-by-step.

Connect: dim the lights, then sit facing each other, gazing into each other's eyes for at least five minutes.

Lay head-to-head on the floor so that your legs form one long line. Nestle your heads on each other's shoulders. The goal is to relax and tune into each other until you can breathe together – it'll take about ten minutes (see tip 59 for more on heavy breathing).

Sit facing each other and redo tip 69.

71

72

Place your hands on each other's chests, **feeling both your hearts beat**. Breathe (see tip 58 for hot panting).

Kiss. Taste each other everywhere. When you become really excited, though, stop and return to tip 69. It's important not to work up too much of a sweat – Tantric-style sex is calm and restful. The point is to keep your head clear while your body gets completely turned on.

73

Almost do it, position 1: Get into your O-Zone –
get on top with your body resting on his chest and
your shins flat on the mattress. He enters you partially
– an inch every five minutes (don't measure!). Lay
still as long as you can. Do your Kegels (see tip 77)
to help him stay erect. When you can't take it any
more, start stroking and kissing (see tip 61 to make
this even sexier), but stop after 20 minutes, letting
your bodies go limp so you don't come.

Almost do it, position 2: He lays on his side (if
you're using condoms, this is the time to put on a
new one) while you lay on your back with your legs
over his and your bodies at a 45° angle. Start again
from tip 69. When you get to step 72, go limp
again (see tip 73).

Now really do it, position 3: Repeat tips 69–72. Then sit on his lap so that you're facing him. This time, let yourself go completely for a total gut-busting orgasm that will stay with you for days.

76

WEEK FOUR: THE INTERCOURSE ORGASM

Time to use the greatest piece of fitness equipment ever invented: a bed.

Anyone who's limber, toned and in shape can make love like a rabbit. But sex is more like synchronized swimming than a 100-metre dash. Timing, in other words, is everything. Bottom line: a strong tongue muscle is only going to get you so far between the sheets. What you need to do is add some exercises and stretches that target the parts of the body called into play during lovemaking, giving you more control over and more intensity during your orgasm.These following high-voltage moves will help boost your performance and give your sex life more pleasure than a lifetime supply of sex toys.

PUMP IT UP

Studies have found that stronger pubococcygeus (PC) muscles make women more orgasmic more frequently and men more likely to experience multiple orgasms. Enough said – here's how to do them.

7

Squeezing your PCs is a bit like wiggling your ears – if you've never focused on the sensation before, finding these muscles may take a bit of time. Here's your four-step guide to gold-standard love muscles:

- The easiest way to locate your PCs is to try to stop your urine flow while on the loo (don't do this more than once a day, as it may irritate your bladder).
- Once you have a general idea of where your PC is, practise the basic Kegel exercise. You can do this in any position, but you'll probably find it most comfortable to do while sitting in a chair or lying on your back. Squeeze your PC, hold for three seconds, then release. Repeat until you can build up to 100 at a time.
- According to Dr Cynthia Mervis Watson, co-author of *Love Potions: A Doctor's Guide to Aphrodisia*, the exercise should be done with your legs slightly apart rather than with your thighs clamped together. You will find that you are drawing your pelvis upwards, but if you find

the exercise tiring, it may be that you're also tensing your buttocks and abdomen; try to isolate only your PC muscles (see next step).

- Place a hand on your abdomen while contracting to ensure that it's relaxed. Inserting a finger into your vagina or placing a hand at the opening also helps identify the movement and confirm that you're squeezing the right muscles.

78 Now use your **pumped-up muscles** to milk him to orgasm. During sex, move your hips very slowly up and down his penis' shaft while squeezing your PCs so you can apply varying amounts of pressure to his organ. Mix in the pelvic moves worked on in tip 47 to get his penis to give you a massage at the same time.

79 **Crush him.** When you're a groan away from climax, let loose by rapidly fluttering your PC muscles – squeezing faster with shorter pauses in between. Flex them five times quickly. The harder and more rapidly you squeeze, the stronger your and his orgasm will be.

30 Boogie slow and easy. Powerfully squeeze your PCs in a constricting manner to push him out. Repeat on the in-stroke, this time squeezing to pull him back in. Push out, constrict, pull in a little and push out and constrict again. When you've developed enough strength, you should be able to **keep it up all night** (get in top shape for this move with tip 45).

31 **Twist to the corkscrew:** With your knees bent, lie on top of your partner, who is on his back with his penis inside you. Resting on his chest, squeeze his penis and slowly circle your hips five times. Stop and release the squeeze. Then squeeze hard again and rotate your hips in the other direction. Continue this cycle until you are both ready to pop.

32 Get him to prod your hot spots. During sex, push down with your PCs to bring the front wall of your vagina down to meet his penis. This helps him **tickle your G-spot**. (Combine this with tip 46 to make this a Gold.)

33 **Push it.** Just add a gentle bearing-down motion to your Kegel contractions during sex, as if you were having a bowel movement. It sounds as sexy as a mental image of Robbie Coltrane naked, but it works.

LET'S GET PHYSICAL

Research has found that the couple who sweat together also sizzle together – they have sex more often and more orgasms when they do it. For an added incentive, do the sexercises naked.

Push-ups tone the chest and arms, making it a cinch to get on top (not to mention fuelling chandelier-swinging abilities). Kneel and place your palms in his hands. Slowly lower and push back up (kisses on the down move make a good incentive). Repeat ten times.

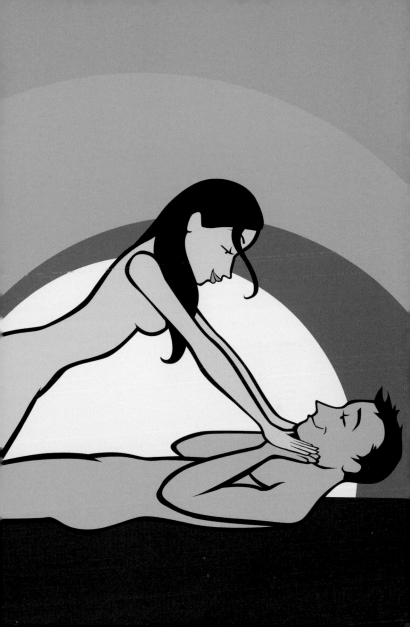

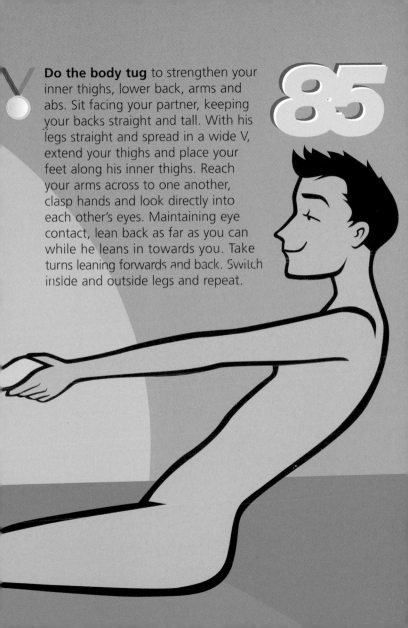

Do the body tug to strengthen your inner thighs, lower back, arms and abs. Sit facing your partner, keeping your backs straight and tall. With his legs straight and spread in a wide V, extend your thighs and place your feet along his inner thighs. Reach your arms across to one another, clasp hands and look directly into each other's eyes. Maintaining eye contact, lean back as far as you can while he leans in towards you. Take turns leaning forwards and back. Switch inside and outside legs and repeat.

85

Do a high-five for a whole-body workout. Stand very close to your partner, face to face. Both of you bend down into a squat, then jump up as high as you can and slap hands (and any other body parts you care to connect) together.

86

Do a better crunch. Instead of tip 50 (the abs workout), place your feet high on his chest (to prevent your back from arching) and contract your stomach, bringing your shoulders closer to your knees. Do two sets of 25 repetitions each.

The pelvic tilt will keep hips, abs and thighs granite hard. Combine this with tip 77 and you'll be a sex engine. Lie on your back with your knees bent and your feet flat on the floor. Rest your arms by your sides and have your partner kneel beside you. As you raise your pelvis slowly off the floor, have him place his hands under you to help you hold the posture, making sure your hips and thighs are in line. Lower your pelvis to the floor and repeat.

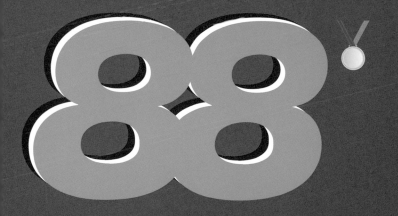

To **strengthen the lower back**, hang your upper body off the bed while he sits on your thighs to stabilize you. Then raise your torso just past horizontal, hold for one beat and lower. Repeat eight times.

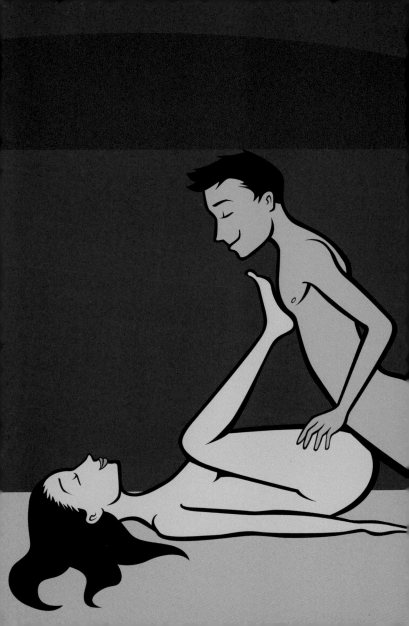

90

Place your feet high on his chest, supporting his body weight. Slowly lower him, bringing your knees to your chest. Push him back to the starting position (penetration is optional). Repeat five times.

Let him be your stretching rack. **Sit with your legs apart**, his feet above your ankles. As you relax forward, he gently pulls your arms to deepen the stretch (repeat twice).

91

PASSION POLE VAULTS

These moves count not only as great sex, but also great exercise. Get ready to do victory laps.

92 Press down*
TARGETS: shoulders
DO IT: Have your partner lie face up underneath you. He penetrates, then moves up and down by doing push-ups that are about half the range of movement of standard ones.

Push back 93
TARGETS: triceps
DO IT: Start from a sitting position on the floor. Lean back, supporting your weight with your hands behind you and your fingers pointing forward. Have your partner slip between your thighs with his knees and hands on the floor, his head just over your shoulder. Pick your bum off the ground. Once he lowers himself onto (and into) you, you do the work. From a bent-elbow starting position, thrust towards him by straightening your arms. Bend again. For more sextension, he can lean against you until you're supporting most of his weight.

94 Love curl*

TARGETS: Biceps

DO IT: Stand about 90 cm (3 ft) away from the wall, with your back to it. Lean your lower back and shoulders against the wall. He should lie on you with his chest to yours, his legs pressed against you and his penis inside you. Scoop your arms around him so your hands are resting against his shoulder blades. He leans back until your arms are extended (take care he doesn't slip out). Slowly curl him back to you. To make it easier, he can put his arms around you and help pull himself up.

Squatter* 95

TARGETS: Quads and hamstrings

DO IT: Have him squat low, leaning back against a wall. Squat over him, making sure you keep your knees bent at a right angle. Move up and down on his penis by pressing with your thighs (if this is too hard, you can give him some of your weight by putting your hands on his thighs).

* For these exercises you can easily switch places so he gets the workout as well.

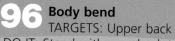

96 Body bend

TARGETS: Upper back

DO IT: Stand with your back to him and your knees bent, leaning slightly forward. Plant your legs firmly with your feet 45 cm (18 in) apart. Have him drape himself over you and penetrate you from behind. Placing your hands on your thighs, support his weight, using your upper back to move you both up and down.

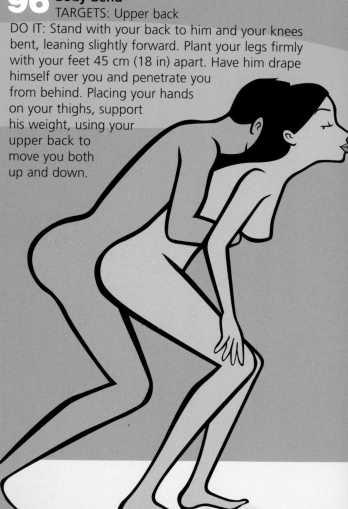

WORK IT

Slip these drills into your regular sex routine and he'll be bending over backwards to please you.

Break orgasm time records. During oral sex or intercourse, have your man support you by slipping his hands under your hips and lifting your pelvis up while you clench your bum muscles.

Put pressure on your abs. Your lower abdomen, just above the pubic hairline, is basically the outside of the inner clitoris. Squeezing the ab muscles intensifies the feeling inside. Do a mini sit-up during sex to tip you over the edge, as it will sandwich your inner clitoris between two hard surfaces (i.e., your tensed muscles and his penis). Note: make sure his penis or finger or whatever hard surface you're using is inserted first.

Open and close your legs in small pumps during sex. Doing this will trigger orgasm in two ways: first, closing your legs makes it easier to clench those thigh muscles (see tips 85, 88, 89 and 96 for strengthening exercises) which actually continue far enough to stimulate your inner clitoris. Second, opening and closing creates friction on the outer visible part of the clitoris and the inner folds of the vulva, which are rich in nerve bundles.

WEEK FIVE: AN ORGASM A DAY

Newsflash: There is a pain-free way to boost looks, improve health, lower stress, make periods pain-free, reduce stress, lift moods, increase confidence and keep you in peak condition.

What is this unknown road to fabulousness?

Sex. And lots of it.

Okay, so you may not wake up with perfectly highlighted tresses, Brad Pitt and a fantastic TV sitcom contract. But it turns out that orgasms don't just feel good. They're also good for you. Because sexual arousal and orgasm involve the interplay of several body systems, it's now known that even a common-or-garden-variety shag does more for your physical wellbeing than a month-long holiday in Tahiti.

These are all the glorious reasons why getting physical will make you look and feel more beautiful (as if you needed an excuse to have more sex!).

THE LOOK OF LOVE

Making love is a painless way to make you look better (and much cheaper than visiting a spa!).

100

Who needs collagen when you have regular sex? A single make-out session can act as a luscious lip-puffer-upper that would make even Angelina Jolie bite her lips.

A snog a day keeps the cosmetic surgeon away. Kissing has been recognized as one of the best facial exercises around. Experts say that all that puckering tones up facial muscles, keeping you looking young and beautiful.

101 102 103

The only cover-up you need for your skin is **a sexy little number**. When Mr Desirable touches you, you get such an explosive rush that it sends blood rushing to the surface, making your heart beat faster and blood pressure rise. It's this rollercoaster of love that makes you positively glow after sex.

Toss away those AHA creams. According to an Ohio University study, orgasm increases your lymphocyte numbers (the cells responsible for fighting physical degeneration) – so regular climaxes could make you remain gorgeous well into old age.

Here's an inexpensive conditioner – sex is known to stimulate the hormones which give your hair a **healthy, shiny sheen**.

A little bit of sex can help you get away with shaving a few years off your age. A Royal Edinburgh Hospital in Scotland study found that sex helps you look between four and seven years younger because it helps you feel more content, sleep better and feel less stressed.

104 105 106

Regular lovemaking increases a woman's oestrogen level, which keeps the skin and vaginal tissues **supple, moist and glowing**.

TRULY
ASTONISHING
SEX
TIPS

1

Eating chocolate can hike up your PEA count. Try smearing chocolate body-paint (available from sex shops) or chocolate syrup over each other's bodies, and then lick it off. Yum!

Scatter **rosebuds** over

your bodies and the bed

before you make love.

The petals will become

crushed between your

sweaty bodies,

gorgeously scenting

your sex. Who said life

wasn't a bed

of roses?

Ask him to give you a **belly orgasm**. Sit erect on the edge of a chair. Your lover should stand behind you and place his hands, pointing downwards, in a triangle on your abdomen – and rub. You'll feel your ovaries get warm and tingle a bit. Breathe deeply. You'll soon begin to feel a sexy buzz.

Get some **sleep**. One study from an American sleep centre found that women who reported going to bed later than usual  one night were rarely in the mood for making love the next. A possible reason for this is that when you're getting enough shut-eye, your levels of the stress hormone, cortisol, drop. Fatigue gives this hormone a chance to build up, which may erode sexual appetite.

Ahh!

Get him to tickle your **Ahh! zone**. Known as the anterior fornix zone, it's a soft, squashy bump located on the front wall of the vagina, between the G-spot and the cervix. This hot spot has awesome bliss potential – studies show that stroking here helps women to become easily lubricated and experience single or multiple orgasms during sex.

5

6 Wash each other's **hair**. Besides being incredibly sensual (think how good it feels at the hairdresser's), the Kinsey Institute New Report on Sex found that good grooming was even more important to lovers than penis or breast size!

7

Ears are an underrated erogenous zone. The lobe and the small area behind the shell have a hot line to the nerves. Stimulation from a darting tongue or a light, probing finger can be a powerful aphrodisiac – especially when combined with heavy breathing into the ear. Scientists call the phenomenon the auriculogenital reflex, and trace its origins to a nerve in the ear canal. Some men find it so exciting they actually climax from it.

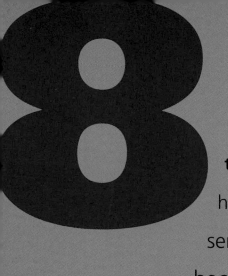

Playing with

temperature

heightens the

sensations

because your

blood vessels

will alternately

expand and contract.

Run an ice-cube

over each other's

hot skin, or spray your

sheets with ice-**cold** water.

Heat things up even more. Take a cup of hot fruity tea to bed with you, sip it and then wrap your mouth around your lover's most sensitive parts. Ask him to do the same. You'll melt with pleasure.

10

Say 'Ooommmm'. In one study, meditation breathing and relaxation exercises significantly raised levels of dehydroepiandrosterone (DHEA), the hormone that revs up our sex drive.

Masturbate. It's a delicious cycle. The more frequent a woman's sexual activity – alone or with a partner – the better her sex life. Research has found that women who pleasure themselves regularly have increased sexual desire, more orgasms, greater sexual and relationship satisfaction and higher self-esteem. Makes you want to give yourself a hand!

Prime your body for a hot and heavy love session. Power squats will build up the muscles that are exercised during sex, giving you added stamina for the main event **(your orgasm)**. Stand up, feet slightly further than shoulder-width apart, arms straight out in front of you for balance. Push your hips and bum back, and bend your knees forward (no further than your toes). Then straighten your legs. Do three sets of 15 reps, three times a week.

13

Tickle the roof of his mouth with your **tongue**.

14

Give
h i s
sacrum a
stroke (and
get him to return
the favour). This
small dent, located just
above the crease of the
bum, (aka the Bermuda
Triangle of love) is extremely
responsive when massaged in a
circular motion with your thumb.

Come – er – prepared. Red-hot lovemaking is a sure thing if you keep your libido on a low boil throughout the day by fantasizing about body-bonding with your lover later on. One study by the Center for Sexual Health at Tulane Medical Center in New Orleans, found that when women have a mental rehearsal for sex, especially if they have a history of orgasm no-shows, their bodies become more sexually responsive within **30 seconds**, once the action really gets going.

16

Resist the urge to make love for a few days, and then set an exact date and time to break the fast. In the meantime, tease each other mercilessly with deep kissing, erotic massage, and light stroking, especially on your favourite hot spots. Sometimes, building anticipation is the most glorious foreplay of all.

17

Learn how to tell a farmer's-daughter joke. Research by the Society for the Scientific Study of Sex found that women who see the **funny side of life**, and are amused by sex-related jokes, are lustier and have higher levels of sexual satisfaction than their more serious sisters.

Call in late to work. The prime time for him to have sex is 9 am. This is when his testosterone level peaks, so physiologically it's all systems go. (You'll probably feel more in the mood, too, as a woman's testosterone cycles often echo her partner's.)

18

With more than **72,000 nerve endings**, your hands are very receptive sex tools. Make the most of every single nerve ending by putting on blindfolds and caressing each other from head to toe, lightly tickling with your fingertips, kneading with your fingers, pressing with your palms, circling with your whole hand and patting gently with the sides of your hands.

Make things **sizzle** by coating his testicles in minty toothpaste before intercourse. The ever-increasing heat sensation this produces will make you both squirm with pleasure. Afterwards, you can lick off any residue (although it won't help to prevent cavities!).

20

21 Give him **a kiss** he'll feel all the way down to his toes. Lie facing each other and press your lips together tenderly *à la* Clark Gable and Vivien Leigh in *Gone with the Wind*. While you can keep the connection for as long as you want, Tantric teachers recommend you hold it for at least seven seconds, in order to experience an all-over glow.

Ignite a secret **hot spot**. Because urine is expelled through the urethra, we don't usually think of this tiny area of tissue just below the clitoris as a sexual point, but Kevin McKenna, PhD, an associate professor of physiology and urology at Northwestern University Medical School, found that it's a possible trigger for orgasm when pressed. It's also a good place to shift your lover's attention, post-orgasm, when your clitoris feels too sensitive for direct stimulation, but you're still in the *mood for pleasure*.

Give each other a body-to-body **rubdown**: ask your man to

lie face down on a soft supportive surface like the

bed or a thickly carpeted floor. Start crawling on top of his

back, rubbing it with the front of your body and

hands. Work your way downwards, finishing with your

breasts wedged in the crease below his buttocks

and your genitals somewhere mid-leg. Your clitoris will

sizzle from the pressure of your movements, and the

sensation of your breasts on his bottom will tantalize him.

If you do this immediately after bathing while your

bodies are still moist, it will make things sensually slippery,

without losing any of the fabulous friction.

23

24

Even the shade of your boudoir or lingerie can affect your rapture rating. In a study at Loyola University in New Orleans, both sexes thought that the **three most erotic colours** (in descending order) were red-orange, dark blue and violet. And the least erotic? Grey.

Style
your pubic
hair. But instead
of a complete shave
with a razor (which can
leave a decidedly un-sexy
itch), trim each other with
electric clippers. Bonus: the vibration
from the clippers will add a delightful
tingle. If he's not sure he wants a haircut
down there, tell him that the shorter the hair,
the bigger his organ will look.

26

Touch

for

your

own

pleasure,

not

your

partner's.

Act like a **vampire** and go for the neck. (Do NOT draw blood!) Gently kissing and sucking the points to the immediate left and right of the Adam's apple drives 1,000 volts of pleasure through the spine.

27

Have a two-in-one orgasm. Some sex experts believe we experience two types of orgasmic sensations – the first is a sharp twinge that occurs when the clitoris or base of the penis is stimulated; the second is a warm melting feeling that happens when the inside of the vagina or the shaft of the penis is aroused to climatic heights. Experience both types, one after the other in a single love fest, and you've had what's

2

called a blended orgasm. He caresses your clitoris until it's almost too sensitive to touch; then he moves his attention to the interior of your vagina. Once you are feeling totally aroused, he moves back to your clitoris. Meanwhile, you are doing the same with his penis, moving from the base to the shaft to the head, and back again. Keep on going for an hour of mind-warping climatic bliss.

Rub a few drops of **lavender oil** into your hair. According to the Smell and Taste Treatment and Research Foundation in Chicago, this scent turns men into lust-crazed beasts (or near enough). Your olfactory turn-on? Cucumbers (no phallic jokes, please).

29

Take your **vitamins and minerals**. According to nutritionists, vitamins B and E and zinc enhance the efficiency of the nervous system, leading to a stronger libido and better orgasms.

Rub his inner **G-spot**. Get him to lie on his back. Sit between his legs and massage the shaft of his penis with one hand, using lots of moisture and a circular stroke. When he's getting close to orgasm, use your other hand to caress his perineum firmly (the hair-free patch of skin at the base of his scrotum). Sit back and watch his toes curl.

Ask your lover to give you a **three-finger** caress. By bringing together the pointer, middle and ring finger of his hand, he will be able to massage every sensitive nerve ending on your clitoris.

③②

33

For a more **intense** orgasm, lie on your back with your head lower than the rest of your body, either by lifting your hips with your hands, with the help of some supporting pillows under your hips, or by positioning yourself so that your head hangs slightly off the bed. This increases blood flow to your brain and changes your breathing, both of which can add to arousal.

Try **dok el arz**, which means 'pounding in the spot'. An ancient Arabian position, it manages to give him the deep penetration that he desires, and your clitoris the attention it craves: the man sits down with his legs stretched out, the woman then places herself astride his thighs, crossing her legs behind her man's back. Lining things up, the woman guides her lover into her. She then places her arms around his neck while he embraces her waist and helps her rise and plunge upon him.

34

Light a
candle.
Undress.
Explore
each
other for
as long
as the
candle
burns.
When it
sputters,
go for
your
climax in
the dark.

THIRTY-FIVE

36

Comedy isn't the only thing that requires good timing. Pencil in sex during the four days following **ovulation** (around the third week of your cycle), when your testosterone levels peak. Studies show that women are more likely to masturbate, initiate intercourse and reach orgasm easily during these days (caveat: they are also more likely to get pregnant).

37 Give each other an alternative orgasm by stimulating one of these acupressure hot spots: use the heel of the hand to gradually increase pressure in the centre of the crease where the thigh joins the front of the torso, rub the area between the mid-thigh and the genitals, or use a forefinger and index finger to massage the temples in gentle circular motions.

Spice up foreplay with the **alphabet game**.

A B C D E F G H I J K L M...

Take turns making capital letters with your

tongue very slowly on each other's genitals.

You might make it to 'M'...

38

39 Pump it up. Your heart, that is. Thirty minutes of aerobic exercise three times a week can do wonders for your sex life – and your orgasm power: studies show it boosts testosterone levels (making you more in the mood for sex), tones cardiovascular endurance (enabling you to last longer), increases blood-vessel diameter and blood volume (making vaginal tissue more sensitive), and improves circulation (making orgasms more forceful).

40 Remember to **breathe**. According to a study by the Center for Marital and Sexual Studies in Los Angeles, most women tend to unconsciously hold their breath during sex, which kills arousal. Instead, try taking slow, regular breaths as you feel your excitement build. The more you can control your breaths, the deeper your orgasm will be.

41

Having a sexy dream at night can make you sizzle during the day. With practice, you can induce a **siesta orgasm** by indulging in your favourite turn-on before you start counting sheep at night.

Feed each other an ambrosial fruit salad. According to the Smell and Taste Treatment and Research Foundation in Chicago, oranges increase penile blood flow by 20 per cent, strawberries spur sexual satisfaction, and spices like nutmeg and cinnamon make you want to do it again and again…

42

43

Play some Harry Connick Jr. A study from the National Opinion Research Center in Chicago found that **jazz** listeners had the most sex. The fluidity of the music also makes you move more rhythmically – especially when you're horizontal.

44

The biggest problem with **orgasms** is that his erupt speedily while yours come at a more leisurely pace. But you can keep him to your rhythm with a tender tug. Using your thumb and fingers, encircle his scrotum (not testicles!) as he nears climax. Squeeze firmly and pull down lightly for a few seconds. He'll groan with ecstatic pleasure if you do it right, with pain if you are too rough. So remember to take it easy – practice makes perfect.

Introduce him to your **breasts**. According to a survey in the *Practical Encyclopedia of Sex and Health*, only 50 per cent of women say they enjoy having their breasts fondled during foreplay – mainly because they're in the hands of men who fumble the ball. Tell him what pleases you by putting your hand over his and caressing the area together.

Exchange **tongue baths** – starting from the fingertips, lick each other's bodies all over, leaving not a single patch unwashed.

Do one thing differently. If you normally nibble his ear, nibble his nipple. If you always end up on top, do it lying on your sides. An Archives of Sexual Behaviour study showed that making **one small variation** in your standard sex routine can help lovemaking to become thrilling all over again.

If you're almost at orgasm and get stuck, sex researchers Julia Heiman and Joseph LoPiccolo have found that deliberately **tensing** your legs, stomach, arms or feet will send you over the edge.

48

Check *Old Moore's Almanac* for the lunar schedule. A report published in the *New England Journal of Medicine* states that women are 30 per cent more sexually active (read: more likely to rip his clothes off) during a **full moon** than at any other time of the month. **49**

50   According to Masters & Johnson, orgasms are really just a sweet release of incredible tension. So boost the intensity of yours by hovering around the 'Ohhh-I'm-almost-there' spot for as long as possible. Get as close to peaking as you can, then relieve the pressure by getting your lover to stimulate a less sensitive area of your body. Repeat until you're **ready to burst**.

Have him lick your **upper lip**. Just about every ancient Eastern sex philosophy claims that this site is the key to a woman's clitoris, and touching it is guaranteed to create

cosmic sparks.

52

Forget oysters. The best aphrodisiac (although, perhaps not the tastiest) is a diet low in lard. The lower your body fat, the higher your levels of testosterone and DHEA. Low blood-cholesterol levels can also reduce plaque build-up in the arteries, increasing circulation and blood flow to the genitals. *Bon appétit.*

Read any **Harold Robbins** book. Rent a sexy video like *Bitter Moon* or *The Lover*. Racy images jump-start your sexual response by raising levels of phenulethulamine (PEA), carnal chemicals that flood your brain when it's buzzed on sex.

The penis has its own **hot spot** just waiting for the right touch. The raphe is a seam, which you can both see and feel, that runs lengthways along the scrotum. Hit his moan zone by lightly tracing your fingers along the line, moving from his bottom forwards and up towards the base of his penis.

Go straight to **sleep**. Sex in the middle of the night, after you've both clocked up a couple of hours' shut-eye, can be much more profound.

55

ZZZZZZ z z

Time your **foreplay**. A Kinsey report found that only 7.7 per cent of women **56** whose lovers spent 21 minutes or longer on pre-penetration fun and games failed to reach orgasm.

For an indirect pleasure prep, gently press the area about 6.5 cm (2½ inches) below your **belly button** for about three minutes. This helps promote blood flow, which stimulates the entire pelvic area. Oh, and you can expect a mind-blowing orgasm, too.

57

58

Ribbed **condoms** are supposed to add to a woman's pleasure. But turn one inside out and those little ridges can do wonderful things to his penis, too (mix in a dab of water-based lubrication to avoid breakage).

Skip the perfume wrist spritz. In Ayurvedic medicine, the ancient Indian science of health and healing, the lower stomach is considered to be the centre of a woman's **sexual stamina**. Dabbing the area with fragrances that are supposed to have aphrodisiac qualities – such as neroli, jasmine, sandalwood and patchouli – will set the scene for a steamy night. As you become aroused, the increased blood flow to your pelvis generates heat in the area, helping to release the fragrance – and unleash your animal magnetism.

59

60°

Get hot – literally. Soak in a warm bath, take a steam or Jacuzzi at your gym, sunbathe (slap on the SPF first), jump up and down until you're sweating, make love on sheets fresh from the dryer. According to a Czechoslovakian study, heat depletes our body's store of stress hormones, making us more in the mood for *l'amour*.

61 Climb **on top** when making love. Experts agree that when a woman is in this position, three marvellous things happen: the forward-facing wall of the vagina (the epicentre of all of her genital hot spots) and the clitoris are more easily stimulated; she can control the angle and depth of penetration more easily; and she becomes more involved in the act of intercourse – all of which add up to a more achievable and impressive orgasm.

x62

Buy a **porn flick**. Yes, YOU. An Archives of Sexual Behaviour study found that women get just as turned on watching erotica as men do. However, since most of the films available are for the male market, you might want to check out Femme Productions, which produce films specifically for women and couples.

Blow his ...mind. Put both of his balls in your mouth at once. Use one hand to circle the top of the sac, and gently pull it down to bring the balls together into a neat swallowable package. Being extremely careful to cover your teeth with your lips, take the sac in your mouth and give him a tongue lashing he'll never forget.

64 Anthropologists call a reddened mouth a **'genital echo'**, a term that includes all body parts with a passing resemblance to a love organ. Drive the point home by applying some bright red lipstick and giving him a blow job (making sure he has a good view).

Equip yourselves with torches and **turn off the lights**. Take turns turning the high beam on each other. Whatever part of the body is lit up has to be caressed for five minutes with the lightee's mouth or hand.

65

66

Sex in the bath can actually dry out your juices. If you're not using latex birth control, add a few drops of oil to the water to keep things lubricated.

67

More **thrusting** does not necessarily mean more fun. The most sensitive nerve endings in the vagina are actually near the opening, so shallow penetration is really better for you. Since this also allows constant stimulation to the head of the penis and, specifically, the hypersensitive frenulum, both of which are squeezed by the vaginal muscles located near the vaginal opening, you won't hear any complaining from him, either.

68

During **foreplay**, pull back your hair so that he can see your face.

Try something new **three times**. The first time, you may be worrying about bending your knees, elbows or both at the proper angle; the second time, you will be thinking about how to make it work for you, but the third time you try you'll probably find that you're able to relax and go with the flow.

Give each other a deep **tonsil-touching** kiss, every time you meet. Experts agree that smooching can be more intimate than sex (which may be why prostitutes often draw the line at kissing). When psychotherapist Sylvia Babbin, PhD, investigated the number of times an average couple kissed, she counted only four-and-a-half pecks per day – including hello, goodbye, good morning and good night.

70

71

Deep-throating is a learned technique. To swallow his penis as fully as possible during oral sex, throw your head back as far as it will go. This opens up the throat and allows you to accept an elongated object without causing your gag reflex to react. Lying on your back with your head over the edge of the bed and breathing through your nose is the most comfortable way to maintain this position.

72 Make him stand to attention. A study at a recent American urology conference established that taking 80 mg of Ginkgo biloba a day can boost his potency (and your pleasure). Seems the herb increases blood flow by relaxing the arteries. But don't expect overnight results – it can take several weeks before you notice a difference.

Move in together. A national survey of Family and Households found that men and women who live together have the most sex, making love more often than non-cohabiting couples, even after they marry.

73

74

Make intercourse **clitoral-friendly**. Research shows that only about 30 per cent of women have regular orgasms from penetration. But when they use something called the coital alignment technique, the odds improve to 77 per cent. Begin with your man on top in the missionary position. He should then slide slightly forward, causing his pelvis to override yours. Instead of thrusting (and completely bypassing the clitoris), you rock your pelvis up while he responds with a downward pressure, so the penis shaft stimulates the clitoris directly, and possibly the G-spot, too.

75

According to the Kinsey Institute, the average man thinks about sex at least once every **half-hour**. Use this knowledge!

Ride a ROLLER COASTER

– or anything else that makes you quake with fear. According to research conducted by psychologist Judy Kuriansky, PhD, **76** for Universal Studios Amusement Park in Florida, experiences that make our stomachs flip over result in a surge of adrenaline and endorphins, which can make us feel more lusty.

Reorganize your bedroom for a more amorous atmosphere. According to **feng shui**, the ancient Chinese art of creating a harmonious living environment, if your bed has a view of the whole room, with nothing blocking the door, your lovemaking will buzz with energy and understanding.

Telling a man you **want** him is the sexiest thing you can do. It packs the same erotic punch as informing him that his team's won, he's won the Lottery AND you've bought him a Harley Davidson. You don't have to be obvious. Simply turn a hello peck into a mini make-out session, and he'll soon get the picture.

78

GO TO THE PUB. According to research cited in *Nature* magazine, one to two glasses of alcohol elevates testosterone levels in women – especially women who are ovulating or on the Pill. But get him to stick to water – booze has the opposite effect on male testosterone **L E V E L S .**

Emptying your bladder makes it easier to stimulate your **G-spot**.

81

Here's a good argument for investing in a **nicotine patch**: a new study reveals that quitters have more orgasms than when they smoked. Tobacco chemicals supposedly constrict blood flow to the vagina and penis, and may lower testosterone levels.

Unlike women, men don't have built-in **lubricants**. Give your hand a lick before caressing his penis to help make things deliciously squishy.

83 Get him to pay as much attention to the minors as the majors. According to a study by the Kinsey Institute, 98 per cent of women say they are as sensitive to having the labia minora, the delicate **inner lips** that surround the clitoris, stroked, as they are to direct clitoral stimulation.

84 Teach him how to multiply. A study from the Health Science Center at Brooklyn found that men can actually learn to climax and keep their erection through three to ten orgasms. The key lies in helping him raise his orgasmic threshold by constantly stimulating him until he's a heartbeat away from ejaculating, then stopping and resting before stimulating him again. The results should be **explosive**.

Get your **tongue** pierced. Apparently the

stud is perfectly positioned to give extra

friction on the most sensitive genital bits

for men and women. Of course,

you could try and create the same effect

by slightly air-drying your tongue

and sticking a frozen pea to it.

Masturbate in front of each other and find out what really turns you on.

86

Make the **missionary** position work for you.

Start by changing the angle of his

dangle so that his penis pushes

87

up against the front wall of your vagina

and tickles your G-spot. This can be done by

slipping a small pillow under your hips or

having your lover place his hands underneath

your hips and lifting your whole pelvic area.

Show yourself. Men like to see naked women, which is why newspapers with topless models continue to flourish (although he STILL says he buys them for their thought-provoking articles). According to the US National Health and Social Life Survey, 50 per cent of men aged 18–44 find watching their partners undress 'very appealing'. Only vaginal intercourse ranked higher.

Plan a **romantic rendezvous** in October. This month sees the annual peak of testosterone in men, which explains why July (nine months later) is the busiest season for obstetricians.

Condoms don't have to interrupt your fun if you make putting them on a part of foreplay. Hold one very gently in your mouth, with the opening facing out. Then, using your tongue to help, gently roll it down your lover's penis with your lips (covering your lips with your teeth will prevent tears to the latex).

91

Access your **sexual chi** (energy) by practising the following ancient Indian breathing technique: block off your left nostril for 15 minutes (if you don't want to use your finger, a piece of cotton wool will do). This should redirect your airflow and ventilate the left side of your brain, which supposedly controls sexual arousal and creativity.

Have him try **The Venus** next time he gives you some oral stimulation. Ask him to alternate between lightly nibbling your clitoris, and flicking his tongue rapidly back and forth over the area. The result is a peel-you-off-the-ceiling kind of orgasm.

92

93 Make him climax faster than you can say, **'Fellatio'**. While sucking his penis, squeeze your thumb and index finger in an up-and-down motion along the ridge on the underside of the penile shaft. Then, using the same two fingers, squeeze under the sac of his balls, with each finger manipulating a ball in the same up-and-down motion (imagine you're milking a cow). You'll produce an orgasm with the intensity of two in a row.

TRIPLE
X
SEX
TRICKS

Section One

Thrill Level

When appropriate, text is rated to determine the Triple X level as follows:

S: Steam it up

E: Edgy and Wild

X: Extreme Kink

Max Out Your Pleasure

Even good sex can become routine. Your body may wobble every time, but it's more because you're using tried-and-tested methods than making a buzz with erotic energy. The good news is that it's easy to add a jolt to routine sex. Just take a stroll on the wild side.

Doing something you've never done before can send your system into overdrive. When you go beyond your limits, you discover hidden turn-ons and new sensations – maybe even a hot zone you never knew you had. Plus, you get the blood-pumping high that comes from being bolder in bed. Your willingness to explore your sexual boundaries will help build intimacy and trust between you and your partner.

When you think about it … is there any reason *not* to have a naughty day?

Pillow Talk

Truly amazing erotic action can happen only when both partners are willing to take risks. Here are eight steps to calm your lover's fears and to get them involved in your secret desires (and liking it!) without setting off perv alarms.

1 Don't beg. Don't grovel. It's not seemly. And it's not necessary. Your best move: Give the relationship a month or two before **breaking out the vibe**.

2 Make sure they know they can **melt you down** sans kink.

3 A weekend away is a good time to get the ball rolling. A **change of scenery** makes people more open to new things.

When the time comes, don't jump right in and unload. Here are four strategies for talking yourself into a wilder sex life, depending on your personality type.

- **If you're shy:** Don't bother talking. Instead, slyly test the waters – see how they react to doing something slightly off from your usual routine. Get into a new position or hold their wrists down. If they act unruffled, they're probably open to at least listening to the idea of doing something a bit unusual. **S**
- **If you're too embarrassed:** Blame it on Freud. Say you had a dream and then describe in detail your favourite wild fantasy. If they're aroused, they'll ask if you want to make it a reality. **E**
- **If you're bold:** Ask about the best sex they've ever had. Or their favourite fantasy. Discovering what they like instead of barking out your wants will make your partner feel less intimidated. Hopefully, if they're half the lover you think they are, they will start asking what *you* like, too. After you tell them, you can show them. **E**
- **If you're a risk taker:** Offer to be their sex slave for the entire day. **X**

Simplify by using a visual aid. You can get a **video or book** with a scene that illustrates your deepest desire. The key, though, is to be specific – 'Do you see that? That makes me really hot.' You can't just watch the film or look at the book and hope they magically get it. **S**

Take a leaf from the *Kama Sutra*. Breaching carnal taboos doesn't sound freaky when it reads like poetry. Instead of asking your lover if they want to try it up the bum, ask if they'd enjoy '**flower congress**'. And rather than wondering if your lover is into light spanking, enquire if they'd like to make the sound 'Hin'. Doesn't that sound much better? **S**

Be prepared for the need for some **damage control**. If you went too far, too fast, here's some phrases to memorize to keep them from running into the night.

- Sorry, you just looked so hot lying/bending/ bouncing like that, I couldn't resist.
- I've never had anyone do that with me before, and I wanted to know what it would be like. You're the first person I've felt comfortable enough to ask.
- Just kidding!
- I thought we could have a naughty little secret between the two of us.

Quit while you're ahead. If they flinched when you climbed on top, it's probably not a great idea to break out the fuzzy cuffs. But even if this isn't for them, maybe they'll like the **flavoured massage oil**.

Rules of the Game

Erotic extras spice up the bedroom, but they can also backfire. Beware of these passion poopers (all players must read the following before starting).

9

Heating it up: Nuking marshmallows, chocolate sauce or honey and **dripping it over each other's body** sounds like a sweet idea, but the results can actually be *too* hot for lovers and cause surface skin burns (same goes for candle wax). Stay in lukewarm territory (if you can dip your finger in without agony, it's probably okay).

Beware **alien invasions**: Don't use any object that's not specifically designed for that part of the body – inserting certain fruit and veggies (see next tip for the exceptions), cooking tools and **candles in the vagina** for instance. But also anal vibrators in the vagina, rubber bands around the penis and so on. You can cause an irritation at the very least and serious injury in a worst-case scenario (do you really want to explain how the vacuum cleaner nozzle got stuck up your bottom?).

Eat your fruit and vegetables: As long as you don't use any food that can break off or get stuck in the vaginal canal, **inserting food** is no more dangerous than inserting a dildo. Things that potentially will not come out are off limits (like grapes). Avoid spicy foods because they could burn. If you use sweet foods near your vaginal area, wash well afterwards to prevent yeast infections. Anything with oil in it (such as chocolate or whipped cream) can burn holes in latex birth control.

Check what's in your **lube**. Some aren't safe to use with latex, others will harm silicone toys.

Don't be a blow-hard: If air is blown directly into the vagina during oral sex, there's a risk it'll accidentally create an air embolus – an **air bubble** that blocks the passage of blood in an artery or vein – which could have lethal consequences.

14

Say what you mean and mean what you say. If you tell your lover, **'I just want to tie up your hands'** and as soon as they oblige, you fasten their feet too, they'll never play cops and robbers with you again – you messed with their trust.

15 Before starting, make sure you're **packing the right tools**. Like if they've agreed to let you go knockin' at the back door, have lube ready and waiting. Or if you're filming your action, make sure the camera is charged up.

Only the brave (and probably not too bright) would let a partner render them helpless after a few dates. **Know your partner** before getting tied up. And never divulge personal info to a cyber-buddy.

Before trying anything new, make a **code word** to stop play. This way, if your lover does something too freaky, you can alert them – IMMEDIATELY. Especially if you're all tied up. Make it an attention-grabber like 'Vinegar'. 'Stop' doesn't work because they may think it's of the 'Stop, it feels so good' variety, as opposed to 'I want everything to stop NOW, no more games, scene over, let me outta here!'

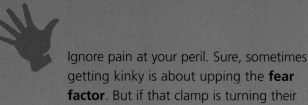

Ignore pain at your peril. Sure, sometimes getting kinky is about upping the **fear factor**. But if that clamp is turning their extremities blue, don't ruin the moment by forcing them to go on. If spanking is part of your play, keep away from kidneys, liver, spleen or tailbone.

18 18 18 18 18

19 19 19

When tying things up, **keep it loose** – circulation is a good thing, especially in all the right parts. Tight scarves and handcuffs can cause numbness; blocking the nose or mouth can make you hyperventilate or induce a panic attack. And never tie anything around the neck. It's also good to have scissors on hand in case Mother shows up unannounced.

Everyone likes sex, but you should never be willing to die for it. HIV and AIDS are more easily spread through anal sex than any other sexual act, so always wear a condom when entering through the back door. Another **rule of the rear** is never to let him double-dip from bottom to vagina without re-rubbering up.

Wash all toys according to manufacturer's recommendations – it'll extend the life of your playthings as well as keep you infection-free.

Bust Out of Your Sex Rut

Five really easy things to get you started on the path to the wild side – and no, you won't need any special equipment.*

Buy some **PVC, leather or suede**. Start small with a glove or a bit of material that you can lie on, wear or rub between your legs or anywhere else that takes your fancy when you make love.

*These all have a guaranteed **S** rating.

Hardcore players use slings purposely designed for some wild fun but you can get the same sensation with a cheap **hammock**. Hang it in a corner of your lounge so it looks like an innocent design feature. Then get **down and dirty** when the lights are out.

TIP: Lying-down hammock sex will just make you feel seasick. Instead, he should stand on the edge while you do **position gymnastics**.

Wrap a silk scarf around your hand. Rub it all over your lover's body, especially back and forth between the thighs and against the crotch. Tie it around his **nuts and bolts**, then tie a large knot with about 30 cm (12 in) of fabric on either end to hold onto. As you ride him, pull on the free ends so that the knot rubs against your love button while constricting his penis and scrotum (which can cause a harder erection). Yee-high!

2 4

Give your guy a demo of **how you touch yourself** when he's not around (it's a No. 1 male secret desire). Start coy with panties on, flicking your fingers through the soft, silky fabric. Payoff one: He'll learn exactly how to press your buttons. Payoff two: You will be the reigning queen in all his future fantasies.

25

TIP: To feel less like a solo act, include him – he can caress your other parts or he can give you his hand and you can use it how you like, making you queen for the day.

Attach a mirror to the ceiling above your bed for some voyeuristic fun.

26

Section Two

What to Wear, What to Wear

What makes on-the-edge clothes feel so extra-special sexy is that you can literally wear them anywhere. There is definitely a supermodel-thin line between what is high fashion and what is something you would find in a porn video – corsets, leather trousers, silky sheer shirts, lacy camisoles, fishnet stockings, PVC skirts and stilettos are just a few examples that have shown up on both sides of the style street.

All of which makes stocking up on your wardrobe a no-sweat, no-angst way to stretch your sexual boundaries. Read on for how to dress up your life.

Seven-Day Sinner

Put this on your daily agenda: Seven days
of dressing up a sexy, sultry you.

MONDAY

AKA Moon Day. Wear
white to work – but
make it **secretive,
sexy, lacy white**. Slip
on a sheer white lace
thong, a garter belt
and a slinky barely-there
white camisole under
your usual work uniform;
you'll feel like the drop-
dead-gorgeous lunar
goddess you really are! **S**

TUESDAY

This is your inner-tramp
day. Do something
naughty that you always
fantasized about, but
your shy side got in the
way. Leave the panties
at home. Instead, wear
head-to-toe leather or
PVC. If your workplace
shuns the Harley-Davidson
look, slip on a leather
thong and bra or 'jumper
bumpers' – small metal
rings that fit around
your nipple to keep
them erect. **E**

27 29 28 30

WEDNESDAY

Mid-week – time to shake off stress, blahs and blues. In short, get a makeover. Hit a salon that can **give your downlow region a new look**. Hot pink dusted with glitter, royal blue with a white trim and lime green are just a few colours to dye for. If you can't get it done professionally, DIY with coloured mousse, gel or hair mascara that washes out with one shampoo (see tips 42–6 for more below-the-belt beauty tricks). **X**

THURSDAY

The week is almost over, so what's a girl to do? Go shoe shopping. Find yourself the maddest, baddest **sky-high stilettos** you can. That extra six inches of height will transform you into a bona-fide dominatrix. To really get the kinks out, make them thigh-high and rubber. Now sashay your hot new self down the street. **X**

FRIDAY

The day of dressing sex-cess. Start the day in red – teddy, camisole, panties and/or bra. Then slip on a silk or velvet shirt that comes off with a quick flick of the wrist (velcro-tabbed or via snaps). After hours, pull out the stops – with cleavage down to here and a long strand of beads dangling in between. Later, just wear the baubles. As things heat up, use them to **tease and please** your lucky lad, running them across his skin and wrapping them around his limbs. Then roll them into a ball and knead his body into a state of bliss. **S**

SATURDAY

Get your booty shaking by giving him a lap dance. Do like the professionals do: Keep your guy fully clothed and make sure you're only wearing a G-string and heels. Absolutely forbid him to touch you (although you can touch him) – it'll give you a sexy, powerful feeling, and seeing your naked body but not being able to touch will make him crazed with desire. Straddle his legs, and wiggle your bottom. **Grind slowly and seductively** to the music, stroking your breasts, and making eye contact. Then mambo your way over to the mattress. **E**

SUNDAY

Pour yourself into a sexy silky negligee and refuse to take it off (think of it as the reverse strip). He has to **kiss and lick** you through the fabric. **S**

Stripped Bare

It's not just what you wear – it's how you take it off. The last thing on his mind will be your cellulite. Promise!

34

Opt for an outfit that accentuates your assets. For example, if your breasts are best, wear a **cleavage-catapulting bustier**. For bottom babes, go for a bum-revealing G-string. **S**

34

34

So you don't **pop out** and knock him on the noggin, slowly **slip down** one bra strap and then the other before undoing your bra. **S**

TIP: Dangle the bra in front of him before dropping it on his lap.

Keep your heels on 'til the last minute. They'll lengthen your legs and make 'em look like something that's just strolled out of a **porn flick**. **E**

37

Wear stockings. You can give him a triple X view by sitting on a chair and lifting one leg at a time, then rolling the stocking s-l-o-w-l-y down with your palms. He'll be **howling oo-la-la**. **E**

38

Drape yourself with **feathery boas or silky scarves** that you can slide off later in the show. **E**

Avoid these fashion don'ts when stripping:

- **Tricky sleeve cuffs** – undo them first so you don't have to stop when slipping your shirt off
- **Tight-necked tops** – you don't want to get stuck mid-strip looking more like a turtle than eye candy
- **Elasticated waistbands** leave very unsexy marks on the skin
- **Back-fastening bras** – front closers avoid any passion-killing fumbling
- **Skip the suspenders** (garters) – lace hold-ups are much less fiddly.

Try switch-hitting by **stripping him**. Slowly undo his shirt. Gently slide it off, kissing and licking his chest. Get down on your knees and remove his shoes and socks. Fondle his penis through his pants as you slip them off. He'll be putty in your hands. **E**

Hair Today, Gone Tomorrow

Tips for sexy head-to-crotch tresses.

Wig out. Try frolicking in the wig section of a department store. The payback for slipping on a totally new, man-made 'do? You can put on a different persona without much effort. Although you may, of course, need a fresh wardrobe to go with your **sexy new alter ego**. E

Dare to bare. Skip the usual bikini line trim and take it all off. Having nothing to cover you and buffer the sensation makes that area hypersensitive. And he'll love the **fuzz-free access** (Translation: More south-of-the-border mouth action for you). **X**

42

The best way to **go hairless** is to take a trip to your local waxing salon and let the professionals handle it. You can turn your expedition into a romp by taking him along. Some places even let him do the honours and **pull the wax**. Yeow – but at least he'll have an idea of what you're going through in the name of eroticism. **X**

If you opt to do it at home, turn it into
a steamy love session. Light candles,
prop yourself on the sink and **spread
your legs wide**. He should take his own
sweet time applying shaving cream. As
he shaves you clean, he can slip in some
teasing moves while whispering in a low,
sexy voice how he's going to give you the
best oral sex of your life. **X**

TIP: Old-fashioned
switch-blades and disposable
razors will give you nicks and
burns. Use a safety razor,
designed for female use.

Get creative and landscape your garden. Trim your hair into any pattern your heart desires: your boyfriend's initials, a lightning bolt, a butterfly – even an **arrow pointing down** (for the benefit of partners with no sense of direction). **X**

He can also go bald. A razor carefully taken to his little man and boys will **make his penis look bigger** by at least an inch or two. Not to mention that it'll prevent work stoppages when you have to pick the hair out of your teeth. **X**

Get the Hole Story

Buy your own personal love stud.

47

A **tongue piercing** can work wonders for oral sex by providing extra sensation to his frenulum (that sensitive area on the underside of his wing-wang) and your clitoris (see www.safepiercing.org for info on keeping it safe when puncturing body parts). **X**

48

Genital piercings also improve sensation. He can get his penis pricked, but rather than wait around for him to get over his wuss attack of letting people with sharp tools down in man-land, you can get a piercing like the '**triangle**' which increases the sensitivity of your clitoris. **X**

49

A **nipple piercing** can turn your little bumps from something that felt OKish-nice to full-fledged erotic zones connected right to your nether regions. **X**

Clothes Encounters

Five fashion accessories no kinkster should be seen without.

Harness: This contraption lets you wear a dildo like a penis. Think of the endless possibilities – you can do him, he can double do you. **X**

5 0

Nipple clamps: If your nips have never felt that sensitive, this will be an eye-opener. You'll feel like there's an amazing livewire connection between your nipples and your clitoris. Start small with just the tip. You can always squeeze more as you play (although you shouldn't leave them in place for more than 20 minutes or you may cause injury). **X**

TIP: Save money and use clothes pegs instead (wood is kinder). Test its tightness on your forefinger and thumb. If it hurts, stretch the metal spring to make it gentler.

52

Vibroclips: These are nipple clips that add an extra kick of vibration. Mmm-mmm good. **X**

53

Nipple ring: Baubles for your bumps. He'll never snub your breasts again.

Orgasm balls: Your best-kept erotic secret. These small balls go clickety-clack inside your vagina all day (they are *not* worn during intercourse), keeping you on tingle alert. The best have built-in vibrators that deliver powerful, leg-trembling pulses hour after – sigh – hour. Your boss will wonder why you're so happy at work. **X**

5

TIP: Work your pelvic floor (squeeze and release your pee muscles) before slipping these in or your balls may go bouncing out at the coffee station.

4

Section Three

Playing with Props

Even the hottest couples can use some fresh, creative ways to keep their lust scorching. Luckily, there are plenty of fun accessories for raising the temperature available from sex accessory websites and stores. All you need is a little know-how and planning to get going. Get ready to lay on a red-hot, good lovin' party!

Get the Kinks Out

Sometimes you need to push the envelope to get the sex life you want.

55

Guaranteed orgasm booster:
Strap on a hands-free vibe and feel your sex life soar. While you and he do the rocket jive, it'll give your – and his – lower regions a tantalizing tingle that will send you on a round-trip to the moon. **E**

56

Guaranteed penis propper: If he tends to droop, a cock ring will keep his package firmly in place. Get one with a built-in vibrator and you'll both be gyrating all night. **X**

TIP: Fit is everything. Go too loose and they do nothing; too tight and he'll never get soft (not as alluring as it sounds after two hours and a trip to emergency).

Guaranteed mood swinger: Using edible body paint, scribble naughty words all over each other's bodies. Then lick it off. Use long strokes running the length of your lover's body. **S**

Guaranteed passion zinger: Pick up an arousal balm and massage it on your most sensitive bits (nipples, inner thighs, genitals … you get the idea). They're spice-packed with mint or cinnamon and will give you a hot tingly sensation all over. Warning: A small amount goes a long way. **S**

Guaranteed position pleaser:
Give any position a little oomph by
stacking up some Liberator cushions
(www.liberatorshapes.com). These
cushions are designed to take the
hassle out of new angles and moves.
Plus you can take them anywhere, so
no more out of bed rug burns. **E**

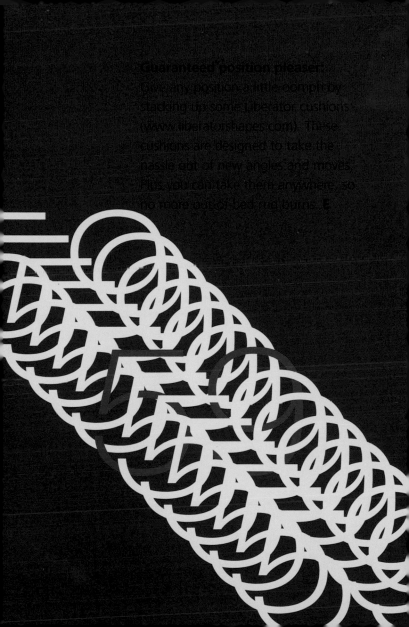

Hot and Handy Tools

How to play with your sex toys.

60

If your vibrator has two speeds, always **start low** so you don't jack the intensity too quickly.

When giving his popsicle a lick, rest your chin on top of a powerful vibrator to add an **incredible buzz**. X

61

62

Turn your scream machine into a sex toy for two. Slip it between your two bodies so it rests against the base of your **pleasure switch** during face2face loving. He'll be able to feel the vibrations while he's inside you. You'll both soon be pulsating with pleasure. **E**

Give him a tickle by stroking a happy trail with your vibrator from his lower belly to his inner thigh. Then lightly trace his **love triangle**, delicately stroking the head of his penis, moving down his shaft and gently circling his balls. Finish off by performing some **mouth magic** on him while grazing his twins and inner thighs with the vibrator. **E**

Dildos

lips

64

Bring in a **stunt double**. When he needs a rest, he can fill you up with a dildo and then touch the base with a vibrator. Silicone is the most realistic material and also best for getting the vibrations to reach their target. **X**

65

Lubes, Oils and Salves

66

Instead of just going in dry on your next blow job, use a gel that not only gives him a **high-pitched tickle** but also gives your tongue a **yummy razzah**. Flavours range from minty to fruity so you can have a taste test. Unfortunately, it doesn't seem to have the same effect when the roles are reversed. **E**

67

Make up your lips with some **vaginal lip gloss** and show him your best smile. He'll swoon over the different flavours and scents (and hopefully want to spend the whole night sampling them). **E**

TIP: Don't reapply the gel in an attempt to go the distance – it'll make your mouth feel like it's been to the dentist.

68

Smear some fruit-scented balm on your nipples and you'll want to skip dessert and head straight to bed. These **zesty creams** warm to the touch and taste heavenly. **E**

69

Pour massage oil directly onto your lover's skin instead of on your hand first, as you would during a regular massage. He'll ooze from the sudden feeling of the **cool massage oil** and then the warming sensation of your hand rubbing the oil in. **E**

TIP: Massage oil is sticky so lighter is better (the last thing you want is a thick, slick coat you can scrape off with your nails). Also, use old sheets.

Anal Beads

Make it easy to go in or out by **lathering up** with plenty of lube. It's easier to pull out if you push down with your bottom muscles (as if going to the toilet). **X**

70

Don't get the **bum's rush** losing your beads. If your trinket doesn't have a ring or handle on the end, leave one or two beads outside the opening so you can pull them out. **X**

71

Timing is everything. Send your lover into a tailspin by s-l-o-w-l-y pulling the beads out during orgasm (they'll have to let you know when blast-off is, so you can start pulling). **X**

72

On the Menu

Put a little kink in your sex diet.

Have a feeding frenzy. Make an **edible passion shopping list** and then send your lover to pick up the booty. Suggestions: cake icing tubes to write on each other with, mints or pop rocks to tuck into your mouth for effervescent oral sex, ice cream to dab on and lick off hot bits, donuts to ring around his erect penis and nibble off, and Champagne for lapping out of your concave places. **S**

73

TIP: Chocolate does not wash off skin easily and leaves embarrassing brown streaks.

74

For chocolate lovers: When his penis is soft, run an ice cube over it and then cover it with **chocolate syrup** that hardens (available at any supermarket). Just make sure you suck instead of bite! **S**

Household Goodies

Skip the toy store – here are nine things you have around the house to push your sex life to the edge.

75

A **silk scarf** can double up as a blindfold or an impromptu hand and leg truss so you can have your wicked way. **S**

76

A **ruler** or **flat-headed hairbrush** will transform you into the impatient teacher ready to discipline a disobedient student (or vice versa). **X**

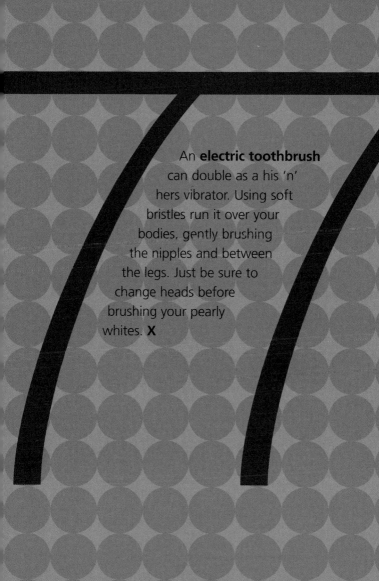

An **electric toothbrush** can double as a his 'n' hers vibrator. Using soft bristles run it over your bodies, gently brushing the nipples and between the legs. Just be sure to change heads before brushing your pearly whites. **X**

Have a dust up with a **feather duster** – you can use it to apply honey dust or icing sugar to various body parts and then lick off your dirty work. **S**

Or pluck out just **one feather** to tickle your lover's bottom hole. **X**

Wrapping **sheer, silky stockings** around your hands like gloves will turn your hand 'job' into a pleasure. It's easier on you than using a dry hand and the sensuous fabric will make him crumple. **S**

81 Make an impromptu cockring by scrunching a **fabric hairband** around his penis base (not *too* tightly). It'll keep him in a state of suspended lust and the fabric will give a pleasure nudge to your love centre. **E**

Light an **unscented, white candle** (perfumes, colourings and beeswax all make the candle burn hotter) and tilt it above your lover's body to allow a single drop of hot wax to land on the skin at a time. For extreme thrills, alternate between hot wax and ice and slip on a **blindfold** so everything comes as a sexy shock. **X**

82

TIP: If you're planning below-the-belt drippings, shave first or die.

Set a **camera** on self-
time to take sneaky
snaps of you two getting
it on. If it's digital, you
can download the pics to
your computer and even
alter the images to make
your own private x-rated
blog paradise. **X**

83

Section Four

Tease Please

The fun starts here. You don't have to be into S&M to experience the pure erotic thrill that comes from playing tie-up games with your lover. Flexing your dominatrix muscles and calling the foreplay shots is a powerful turn-on. On the other hand, simply be a prisoner of your lover's lust and let them have their wicked way with you.

Don't worry. You won't need special equipment to get started (that's for later!). Just pack your imagination and the desire to romp rough. But remember: Sex, no matter how wild, is supposed to be about loving it up – not drawing blood!

How to Be the Boss in the Bedroom

Don't be skittish about telling your lover exactly what you want.

84

Play **Lover, May I?**. The rule of the game: No touching without asking, 'May I touch/lick/suck/bang your…' (insert favourite bit here). Naming the parts means you'll be forced to mouth off like porn stars. You can add a dom tone by establishing your **chick-in-charge** position and occasionally denying him access. **S**

Practise **verbal bondage** by telling
him to act like a statue. He holds his hands
up, each fingertip touching the opposite fingertip.
Put a penny between each pair of fingertips so he's
holding five pennies. Now order him not to let a single
one drop, on pain of punishment (such as he has to
be your **sex slave** for one day) and then go
to work ravishing him.

TIP: This works best on
a hard floor so you can hear
the coin drop – which it
definitely will. **E**

85

Don't give him a chance to think – straddle him, pull his head back with a tug of his hair and just take him. Use **tough-love techniques** like naughty ear and neck nips, pushing your fingertips deep into the fleshiest part of his buttocks while he thrusts, pulling his face to your breasts as you hit your passion peak. He'll be delighted with your diva moves. **E**

Swap roles and have him put on the **bad-boy persona**. Say you want him to take you on the rough side. His script: To pounce and hold you down, then breathe in your ear how hot he is (his talk should be part Romeo, part porno). Sex up the scenario by pretending to push him away, you **damsel in desire**! **E**

Lie back on the bed with your arms outstretched and purr, **'Do whatever you want with me.' S**

Always **cuddle** after. **S**

See No Evil

Give new meaning to the phrase, 'love is blind'.

Once you've got your man blind, treat him to a slew of new sensations: gently nibble him, trail your **hardened tongue** over his body, tickle him with your fingers, swish your hair over his bits. He'll have no idea where you'll strike next. At the crucial moment, climb on top, hold his face and make him stare right into your eyes as you **ride him to oblivion**. E

TIP: Start low-key and use your hands instead of a blindfold to cover his eyes.

90

91

Tantalize him by slipping a scarf over his orbs and teasing him any way you desire. You're in **total control** of his pleasure, so pull out the stops by stimulating him with sensual props (see Section 3 for ideas). Mix up your touch to keep his **temperature** high. **E**

TIP: Don't forget to take a turn behind the veil so he can have fun ordering up your moans and groans.

Have a fox hunt. You both get naked but one of you wears a blindfold (a scarf will do). The other hides. The **masked lover** gets on hands and knees (to avoid tripping or bumping into things) and has to find the other. The hider can pop up out of nowhere, only to disappear in the next instant. **Tally-ho! E**

Get Fit-to-Be-Tied

How to tie one on and feel no pain.

When you're ready to be bound for love, don't reach for the **handcuffs** unless they're specially made for sex play (fur-lined, for example). The metal versions are more likely to bruise your wrists or – worse – break mid-play. The beginner's best is nylon because they open easily, and are affordable and comfy to wear. DIYers can use scarves, bandanas, stockings, a tie or cotton rope.

TIP: Always tie them loosely so you can get out easily in a pinch.

94

If your bed has
no posts, you can wrap
ropes around the legs of the bed
and **spread-eagle your lover**. Or tie
his wrists behind his back and then
to his waist. **X**

Have him **tie your hands and feet** together
and then set you up on your elbows and
knees. He then comes from behind to
worship you mercilessly while you
love every minute of it. **X**

Tie him to a chair and then do a **striptease** followed by a **lap dance** (see tip 32 for how-to). **E**

96

Tickling is **terrific torture** that's especially good if he's all tied up with nowhere to go. Run a feather up and down his body until he begs for mercy. **S**

TIP: When he returns the favour, you may discover you're one of the few lucky women who can get tickled to orgasm.

97

TIP: To really put you into a Saturday night fever, he can switch-hit between an ice cube and a fur-covered mitt on your globes.

98

One tormenting trick he can try on you: He ties you spread-eagled to the bed and rests a vibrator on your push button. While he plays with your breasts, you'll be **writhing like a disco dancer** trying to get the buzz exactly where you want it. **X**

Spank Amateurs

It's swattin' time.

Next time you're smack bang in the heat of things, whisper to your partner that you've been bad and you need a spanking. Add a little **bottom squirming** to emphasize your point. **E**

If you plan to be in charge of the smackdown, make sure he knows. Wear **black thigh-high boots** and a **naughty teddy** to set the mood and then tell him he's been misbehaving and needs to be punished. **X**

Get your lover in **spanking position**. The classic pose for her is bent over his knee with her bottom up for a good licking. If he's on the receiving end, he should lean against a waist-high object (table, bed, car) that'll brace him against her thumps.

Spank it like a pro. Your lover's bottom is not your boss's face, so keep your everyday aggressions out of the bedroom. **Start by rubbing** (you can rub one or both cheeks, but only smack one cheek at a time). Don't worry, before you know it, they'll turn the other cheek. After you smack it, rub the area a little bit, not only to soften the blow, but also to show that it was an affectionate butt whooping.

Hit the **bull's-eye**. The hind end's sweet spot is the well-padded bit where cheek meets the thigh. Spank close to the genitals and they'll indirectly get stimulated, sending your sugarbaby into sweet oblivion. **E**

Keep the rhythm. The winning beat: two light smacks, one slightly harder, then three light smacks and one hard one, and repeat. This build up will deem you **Spank Master**. E

End with a bang. Spanking sessions end when the one on the receiving end cries, 'Uncle'. Ask, '**Will you be good now?**' If they agree, lay off, kick back, and let them show you exactly how good. E

Section Five

Pushing the Limits

Same time, same place, same position?
Some fun and games can shake you
out of your ho-hum routine.

Most of these tips take some preparation.
But working a kinky act is never a quickie,
which is why doing it makes you pant with
lust. Deciding what secret desire you want
to play out, stocking up on the equipment
and planning the scene together are all part
of the buzz. So shelve your inhibitions
and get ready to vice things up with
these sextreme suggestions.

Bottom's Up

The ins and outs of rear-ending in the bedroom.

106

It's not a vagina; it doesn't secrete fluid. Unless you want to see your lover leap up and dig their nails into the ceiling, **grease up**. Silicone lubes (versus glycerine ones like K-Y and some versions of Wet and Astroglide) are slick and slidey and stay that way longer.

For obvious reasons, it's a good idea for the partner on the receiving end to take a trip to the toilet (and possibly the shower for a **soapy wash**) before anything gets started.

107

08

You don't have to go for a deep plunge. The highest concentration of nerve endings is around the anal opening itself so just inch your finger or tongue in for a quick **skinny dip** while playing at the other end. **E**

The key is re-lax-ation. Start off with a long, **warm bath**, or better yet, give your lover a few **teeth-numbing**, stupefying orgasms before you head 'round back. **S**

109

If you do decide to do a full bottom bungee jump, follow these four steps for a smooth dive.

• **Get cheeky.** Don't lunge straight for the hole. Spreading and softly squeezing and rubbing your lover's derrière will put them in a relaxed, receptive mood. **S**

• **Test the waters** with one, then two (well-lubed) fingers before you let little Johnny jump in. Work your way up very gradually, gently stroking the region right around the opening, then pushing gently at the centre but not actually penetrating. **E**

- **Get into position** – puppy style is easiest for newbies. **E**

TIP: Hopping on top means you can call the shots but it tends to tighten your butt muscles, making penetration tougher.

- Once the head of the penis is in, **stop and relax** for a couple minutes, to get used to the sensation.

Turn him into a love fool by **poking his prostate** (on the rectal wall on the side toward his genitals). **Lick his lollipop** at the same time and watch him drool. **X**

1 & 2

Try a little **rim around the rosie** with your tongue. Make your tongue flat and hard for the most **yum-gasmic** sensation. **X**

**Toy with
your bottom.**
Use a small dildo
or vibrator specifically
made for anal insertion
(they're flared so won't get
sucked in and lost in your no-
man's land) or **butt plug** (a small
flared stopper that's inserted and
sometimes
left in the
bottom) or
anal beads (think cheap
plastic necklace – see tips 70–2).

114

Use lots of **hands-on techniques**. While making a pass at the back door, work in a double play by slipping your other hand around the front end. He can use fingers or a vibrator on her orgasm lever or navigate his way down her vaginal canal, bumping along the bottom wall to buoy up the **pleasure waves** while she can pull on his boys or give his wood a jiggle. **X**

Fantasy Island

How to make your dreams come true.

Make sharing time easier when it comes to your erotic whimsies. Scribble your **top three fantasies** on a piece of paper and number them from one to six. Toss a die and pick whichever number comes up with the promise you'll act it out. **E**

Act out an **orgy *à deux***.
Close your eyes or use
blindfolds and work all your
digits and tongues at the same
time: play with nipples while
using your mouth down below;
slide a dildo in from behind
while using a vibe mitt in front.
It'll feel like a gangbuster. **S**

If the thought – but not the reality – of adding another
girl to your love dance makes you liquefy, arrange to
get an at-home rub-down while he watches. You'll get
warmed up with a **mah-vellous massage** and plenty
of material to fire your engines later. **E**

Get into the Role

Throw your own private fancy dress party.

Five things to put in your closet right now: **X**

HER	HIM
Corset	**Pirate outfit**
Any uniform (nurse, maid)	**Any uniform** (cop, firefighter)
Catsuit (fishnet, latex, silky material)	**Leather trousers**
Cheerleader	**Football player**
Vamp (think cleavage and tight)	**Male stripper** (think thong)

118